Hooray for Sheep Farming!

A Bobbie Kalman Book

Crabtree Publishing Company

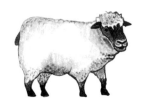

Hooray for Sheep Farming!
A Bobbie Kalman Book

**For Karl and Priscilla Baker and Rambo
from baa, baa, Baa-bbie**

Editor-in-Chief
Bobbie Kalman

Writing team
Bobbie Kalman
Allison Larin
Niki Walker

Managing editor
Lynda Hale

Editors
Niki Walker
Greg Nickles

Text and photo research
Allison Larin

Computer design
Lynda Hale
Campbell Creative Services
 (cover type)

Consultants
Karl G. Baker, D.V.M.
Ontario Agri-Food Education

Illustrations
All illustrations by Cori Marvin

Special thanks to
American Wool Council/American Sheep Industry Association;
Sandra Hawkins of Ontario Agri-Food Education; Julie Scarlett of the
Ontario Sheep Marketing Agency; Karl and Priscilla Baker; Brian Dibble;
Sarah Parker; Amanda Vernal and Allison Vernal

Photographs
AGstockUSA/Patrick Cone: page 15
Peter Crabtree: pages 13 (both), 23 (all), 24 (all), 25 (both), 28, 29
Giraudon/Art Resource, NY: pages 6-7
National Museum of American Art, Washington DC/
 Art Resource, NY: page 14 (detail)
Ontario Sheep Marketing Agency/Philina English: page 14 (bottom)
Photo Researchers, Inc.:Bill Bachman: page 17;
 Gregory G. Dimijian: title page; Jack Fields: page 16;
 John Eastcott & Yva Momatiuk: pages 4, 8; Kees van den Berg: page 18
Positive Images: Karen Bussolini: page 9; Arleen Lorrance: back cover
Milton Rand/Tom Stack & Associates: page 12
James P. Rowan: page 22

Printer
Worzalla Publishing Company

Color separations and film
Dot 'n Line Image Inc.
CCS Princeton (cover)

Crabtree Publishing Company

350 Fifth Avenue
Suite 3308
New York
N.Y. 10118

360 York Road, RR 4,
Niagara-on-the-Lake,
Ontario, Canada
L0S 1J0

73 Lime Walk
Headington
Oxford OX3 7AD
United Kingdom

Cataloging in Publication Data
Kalman, Bobbie
 Hooray for sheep farming!

(Hooray for farming!)
Includes index.

ISBN 0-86505-655-2 (library bound) ISBN 0-86505-669-2 (pbk.)
This book introduces the farming of sheep for wool, covering such
aspects as shearing, lambs, sheep dogs, wool processing, farm
maintenance, and the proper care of sheep.
1. Sheep—Juvenile literature. 2. Wool—Juvenile literature.
[1. Sheep. 2. Wool. 3. Farm life.] I.Title. II. Series: Kalman, Bobbie.
Hooray for farming!

SF375.2.K35 1997   j636.3'145   LC 97-31449
                                                          CIP

Sheep farming for "ewe"

Raising sheep for wool

Sheep farmers are called **shepherds**. Shepherds care for sheep and keep them healthy. Some shepherds raise sheep for meat, which is called **mutton**. This book is about shepherds who raise sheep for their wool. Wool grows all over a sheep's body.

Wonderful wool

Sheep's wool is used to make blankets, carpets, and clothing. It weighs less than other fabrics and soaks up and holds water easily. A person wearing a wool coat in rain or snow would not get as wet as a person wearing a cotton one. Wool also keeps people warm.

Hooray for sheep farming!

The next time you put on a woolen scarf or sweater, shout "Hooray for sheep! Hooray for sheep farming!"

Sheep farming

Sheep were the first animals **domesticated** by people for food. Domesticated animals are animals that have been taken out of the wild and tamed. Humans must feed and care for them. Cows, horses, chickens, pigs, and pet dogs and cats are other examples of domesticated animals.

Shepherds of long ago

Long ago, there were no sheep farms. Shepherds cared for the sheep of several families. A shepherd wandered the countryside with the sheep while they ate grass in meadows. The shepherd also protected them from wild animals. Being a shepherd was a lonely job.

Specializing in meat or wool

In the past, a sheep was raised for both its wool and meat. Even its fat was used for making candles and soap. Today, sheep farmers **specialize**, which means they raise their animals only for meat or wool.

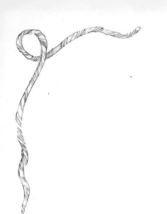

Ewes, rams, and lambs

A male sheep is called a **ram**. Female sheep are **ewes**. Sheep under one year of age are called **lambs**. A group of sheep is a **flock**.

Call me Ram-bo!

Rams are larger than ewes, and sometimes they fight. Each ram wants to prove that he is the strongest so that he gets to **mate**. Ewes and rams mate in order to make lambs. A ewe has one or two lambs at a time. She can have lambs once or twice each year.

A lamb is born

When a lamb is born, it must be kept warm. The shepherd weighs the lamb and **vaccinates** it. A vaccination is medicine given with a needle. It helps the lamb fight sickness. Lambs grow quickly. At about ten weeks old, they are **weaned**. They stop drinking their mother's milk and learn to eat solid food.

Back to the flock!

The shepherd puts a numbered tag on each lamb's ear to show which lamb belongs to which ewe. A new lamb and its mother are allowed to join the flock when the farmer is sure that they are strong and healthy. The lamb knows which ewe is its mother. It goes to her when it is afraid or hungry.

At the sheep farm

Sheep spend most of their time outdoors. Farms have one or more barns where the sheep are kept when they have lambs or when they are sick. The **shearing room** is in the barn. It is where the sheep have their wool clipped off, or **sheared**, each spring.

The pasture

Sheep spend most of their time **grazing**, or eating grasses and plants, in the **pasture**. A pasture is a large, open field where grasses and other small plants grow.

The drylot

The **drylot** is an area of the farm that has no grass. The shepherd moves sheep there when they have eaten enough grass for the day. He or she does not want the sheep to eat too much grass. If they do, they could get **bloat**, an illness that can kill them. The shepherd puts other foods such as hay and grain in the drylot. He or she makes sure that the sheep get enough of these foods to stay healthy. There is also fresh water for the sheep to drink.

barn

pasture

shearing room

drylot

11

Feeding the sheep

Sheep spend a lot of time eating grass and clover in the pasture. A pasture always has a fence around it so that the sheep cannot wander off and get lost.

Different grasses

Some kinds of grass grow in the spring, and some grow in the summer. Other grasses grow in the fall. A pasture must have many kinds of grasses so that the sheep have plenty of fresh food to eat during each season.

Shepherds feed grain such as corn to the sheep. They also put out large blocks of salt and minerals for the sheep to lick. Sheep need nutrients from these foods in their diet, and they do not get all of them from grasses in the pasture.

Extra food

The grass in the pasture does not always give sheep all the nutrition they need. The shepherd sometimes gives sheep extra food to keep them healthy. He or she fills troughs with hay and grain for the sheep to eat. Sheep also need fresh water. The shepherd makes sure there is always plenty of clean water to drink.

Winter feeding

During the winter, grass does not grow. The shepherd must put out much more grain and hay for the flock in the pasture. He or she also feeds the sheep in the drylot.

14

The shepherd loads his truck with bales of hay and drives the food out to the pasture. One sheep is so anxious to eat that it nearly knocks over the shepherd!

Sheep dogs

Many shepherds have **sheep dogs**. These dogs are trained to help care for a flock. **Herding dogs** help herd the sheep. They gather them into a group and guide them from one place to another. **Guard dogs** protect the sheep from wild animals while they are in the pasture. Some dogs do both jobs.

16

Herding dogs

Herding dogs chase sheep into a group by running around them. They push the flock in the direction the shepherd wants them to go. The dogs know not to bark at the sheep while herding them. The sheep would become scared and hard to control if they did.

These dogs are working together to herd this large flock of sheep into the drylot. The sheep are on their way to be sheared.

Guard animals

Guard dogs stay in the pasture with the flock. They watch over the sheep and protect them from coyotes, wolves, and other wild animals. They also stop people from stealing sheep. Shepherds once had to do this job themselves. They could not take their eyes off their flock!

This donkey has lived with the same flock since it was a baby. It thinks of the sheep as its family and guards them from predators.

Donkeys and llamas

Some shepherds do not use dogs to guard their sheep. They use donkeys or llamas instead. These animals are the natural enemies of coyotes and wolves. When these **predators** come near the flock, the donkey or llama chases them away.

llama

19

Wool types

Different types of sheep grow different kinds of wool. Some grow **fine wool**, some grow **medium wool**, and others grow **coarse wool**. Fine wool is very thin and soft. Coarse wool is thick and rough. Medium wool is between fine and coarse wool.

Choosing sheep

The illustrations on these pages show just a few types of sheep that shepherds can raise. Most shepherds raise sheep that grow medium wool. Medium wool is easier to sell because it can be used in many ways.

Look at the strand of wool yarn above each column of sheep. It will show you which type of wool the sheep beneath it grow. Look at the pictures and names of the sheep. Use them to identify the sheep throughout this book.

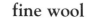

fine wool

Merino

Rambouillet

Debouillet

medium wool

coarse wool

Suffolk

Border Leicester

Corriedale

Lincoln

Oxford

Romney

21

Shearing sheep

A sheep's wool grows throughout the summer, fall, and winter. By the time spring comes, the wool is very heavy for the sheep to carry around. It must be sheared off. Shearing does not hurt the sheep. It is like getting a haircut.

How a sheep is sheared

A person who shears sheep is called a **shearer**. The shearer clips the wool as close to the sheep's skin as possible.

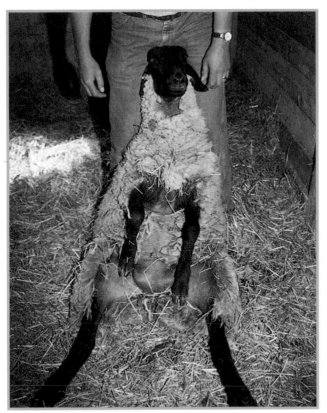

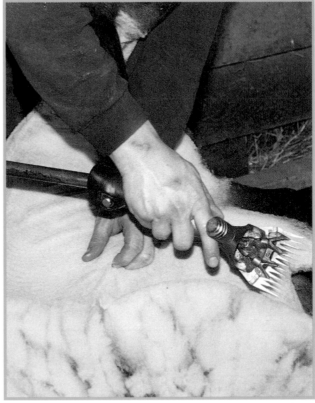

(*top left*) Before the shearer can begin, he or she **rumps** the sheep, or flops it onto its rump. A rumped sheep cannot run away.

(*above*) The shearer uses electric clippers that cut the wool without cutting the sheep's skin. The shearer keeps the clippers clean so that no germs are spread from one sheep to the next. The clippers are cleaned with **disinfectant**, a mixture of chemicals that kills germs, diseases, and insects.

(*left*) The shearer begins shearing at the sheep's belly.

(opposite, top left and right) The shearer tries to clip the wool off in one sheet, which is much easier to handle than several small pieces.

(opposite, bottom left) All this wool came from one sheep! A single sheet of wool is called a **fleece**.

(opposite bottom right) The fleece is put into a **jig**, a device used for tying wool into a bale.

(above) The bale is tied with a string so that it is easier to handle.

(right) Sheep are put in the drylot after they are sheared. They often run and jump around because they feel so much lighter without their wool.

Keeping sheep clean

The shepherd has to do much more than just feed and shear the flock. He or she must keep the sheep clean and healthy so that they will grow good-quality wool.

Dirt jackets

A sheep's wool can get full of dirt in the pasture, and flies often lay their eggs in it. Sheep farmers who do not want the wool to get too soiled put jackets on their sheep. The jackets keep dirt, seeds, branches, and flies from getting into the wool.

Sheep dip

Sheep get upset when there are insects on them because insect bites hurt their skin and cause it to itch. Insects that live in a sheep's wool can also make the animal sick. A shepherd dips sheep into **sheep dip** to kill the insects. Sheep dip is a pool of chemicals called **insecticides**. The sheep walk through the pool so that their wool gets soaked. Sheep may not enjoy getting wet, but they feel much better when there are no insects living in their wool!

Healthy sheep

Shepherds want their sheep to be healthy. Unhealthy sheep can become weak or ill and even die. Every spring the farmers give their sheep shots to protect them from diseases, infections, and **internal parasites**. Internal parasites are tiny creatures that live in animals' bodies and can make them sick.

Checking the teeth

At the front of their mouth, sheep have only bottom teeth. They have a thick pad on their upper jaw instead of teeth. Over time, a sheep's bottom teeth wear down from pulling grass out of the ground to eat. Shepherds examine their older sheep's teeth once a year to make sure they are still long enough to pull grass from the pasture.

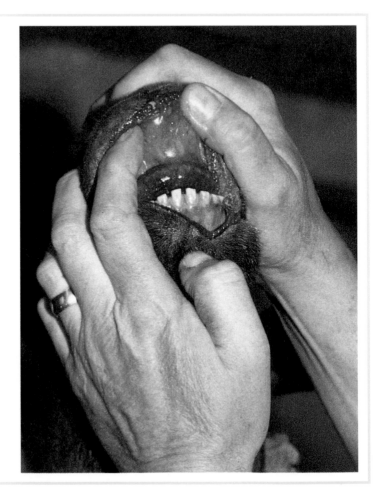

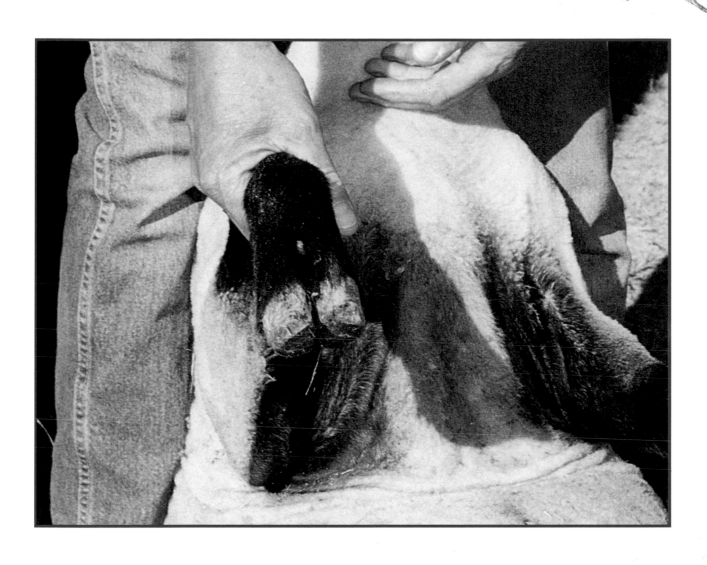

Checking the hoofs

The shepherd examines the sheep's hoofs often to make sure they are not injured. Sometimes a stone gets jammed into a hoof. The hoof gets sore, and it becomes difficult for the sheep to walk on it. The shepherd must remove any stones so that the sheep can walk properly.

From wool to yarn

Wool grows on a sheep the way hair grows on a person's head. A sheep's wool coat is made up of millions of tiny fibers. After wool is sheared off the sheep, many things must be done to it before it can be used by people.

30

Washing the wool

Fleece is **scoured**, or washed, in a tank of warm water and soap. Big rakes swish the wool through the water. The fleece is then wrung out between big rollers. It is dried with hot air in the **drying chamber**.

Carding the wool

After being washed, wool is **carded** to untangle its fibers. A **carding machine** combs the fibers so they lie in the same direction. Its **cylinders** are covered with fine wire teeth. Each one is a different size and spins at a different speed.

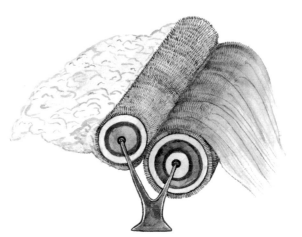

The tangled wool runs through these two carding cylinders. The cylinders comb the wool fibers into a thin, neat web.

Spinning the wool into yarn

The wool is like a thin web when it is removed from the carding machine. This web is **spun**, or twisted, into one long piece of yarn. The yarn is wound onto a spool to keep it from getting tangled.

What do we make with yarn?

Woolen yarn is **woven** into fabric on big machines called **looms**. Some factories use this fabric to make wool carpets and blankets. Some make wool clothing.

Wool hats and sweaters are wonderfully warm!

Sheep farming words

bale A large bundle of wool tied tightly with string

card To separate or comb fibers of wool

drylot A fenced area of the farm that has no grass

fiber A single strand of material such as hair or wool

fleece The single sheet of wool that is sheared off a sheep at one time

flock A group of sheep

herd To gather sheep into a group and lead them

lamb A baby sheep

mate To make babies

pasture A large, fenced field where grasses and other small plants grow

predator An animal that kills and eats other animals

shear To clip off a sheep's wool

shearer The person who clips a sheep's wool

shearing room A room in a barn where sheep's wool is clipped

shepherd A sheep farmer

wean To make a baby used to food other than its mother's milk

weave To lace threads or yarn together in order to make cloth

Index

2 3 4 5 6 7 8 9 0   Printed in the U.S.A.   6 5 4 3 2 1 0 9 8